Helping Children See Jesus

ISBN: 978-1-933206-16-5

PRAYER
New Testament Volume 9: Life of Christ Part 9

Author: Ruth B. Greiner
Illustrator: Frances H. Hertzler
Colorization courtesy of Good Life Ministries
Typesetting and Layout: Morgan Melton, Patricia Pope

© 2018 Bible Visuals International
PO Box 153, Akron, PA 17501-0153
Phone: (717) 859-1131
www.biblevisuals.org

All rights reserved. No part of this publication may be reproduced, stored in a retrieval system or transmitted in any form by any means, electronic, mechanical, photocopy, recording or otherwise, without the prior permission of the publisher, except as provided by USA copyright law.

RELATED ITEMS

To access related items (such as activities, memory verse posters and translated texts) please visit our web store at shop.biblevisuals.org and enter 1009 in the search box on the page.

FREE TEXT DOWNLOAD

To access a FREE printable copy of the teaching text (PDF format) in English or other available languages, enter S1009DL in the search box. Add the item to your cart, and use coupon code XTACSV17 at checkout. Once your order is processed you will receive an email with a link to the free download.

For the eyes of the Lord are over the righteous, and His ears are open unto their prayers. 1 Peter 3:12a

Lesson 1
THE PHARISEE AND THE PUBLICAN

Scripture to be studied: Matthew 23:1-30; Luke 18:9-14; Isaiah 40:19; 44:14-19

The *aim* of the lesson: To answer the questions: (1) What is prayer? (2) To whom should we pray? (3) Who can pray?

What your students should *know*: The true and living God hears and answers the prayers of those who have been forgiven of their sins.

What your students should *feel*: A desire to pray to God.

What your students should *do*: Pray, confessing their sins to God and asking His forgiveness.

Lesson outline (for the teacher's and students' notebooks):
1. Many people pray to idols (Isaiah 40:19; 44:14-19).
2. The Pharisee spoke proudly of himself (Matthew 23:1-30; Luke 18:9-12).
3. The tax collector prayed humbly to God (Luke 18:13).
4. God hears the prayers of those who confess their sins and seek forgiveness (Luke 18:14).

The verse to be memorized:

For the eyes of the Lord are over the righteous, and His ears are open unto their prayers. (1 Peter 3:12a)

NOTE TO THE TEACHER

The Word of God has much to say about prayer. It is important to study and teach the blessed truths concerning prayer. We must experience these truths in our daily lives. Prayer is a priceless privilege. If the power of prayer is a reality to you, teacher, these lessons will live to your class.

The main reason for teaching these four lessons is to help each of your students to learn to pray.

THE LESSON

Who can tell me the name of the ruler of this country? How many of you have ever seen him in person? Have you ever talked to him? Suppose you desire to speak to the ruler of this land. Can you walk right into his home at any time and say whatever you wish? Of course not. He is a busy person. You would have to have a very important reason for wanting to talk to him. And even then you probably would not be allowed into his presence without special permission.

There is Someone who is higher and much greater than any ruler on earth. Who is this One? He is the living God, the Creator of Heaven and earth. He is great and wise and almighty. Does He allow people to come into His presence at any time to talk with Him? And even better than *allowing* people to come, He actually *invites* them to come! The very One who made the world–the trees, grass, flowers, mountains, animals and people–wants people to talk to Him. God, who knows everything and can do everything is always ready to listen to those who talk to Him. Talking to God seems simple enough. Yet numbers of people in the world know little or nothing about true prayer. Others do not know that God has set certain rules that must be followed if prayer is to be answered.

1. MANY PEOPLE PRAY TO IDOLS
Isaiah 40:19; 44:14-19

Many pray but not to the true and living God. Why? Because they do not know Him. The Bible says that some people pray to idols which they themselves have made and trimmed with gold and silver. (See Isaiah 40:19.)

Show Illustration #1

If a man is too poor to buy an expensive gold idol, he may cut down a tree–perhaps a tree which he himself had planted. He will use some of the wood to make a fire to warm himself. He may burn some of that same wood to bake his bread. And he will use the rest of the wood to have a face carved on it. Then, falling down before it, he worships and prays to it saying, "Help me, for you are my god." (See Isaiah 44:14-19.)

He will not stop to think: *This is only a piece of wood. I have burned part of it to keep me warm. I have used some of it to bake my bread. How can the rest of it be a god? Why should I pray to a piece of wood? Can my wooden god hear me?* No, he does not ask such questions. He simply prays to his piece of wood as if it really were a god who could hear and answer prayer. How foolish!

Some men and women climb the steps of temples on their hands and knees. They think that by doing this, their god (it may be a gold one) will hear their prayers. Others write their prayers on paper and fasten them to prayer wheels. They expect that each time the prayer wheel turns, the words of their prayer will be repeated.

Hosts of people believe that if they offer sacrifices to their gods, their gods will answer their prayers. In fact, there have been some who suppose that the true God of Heaven demands a sacrifice before He will hear prayer. But hundreds of years ago a prophet of God (Isaiah) told the people of God (Israel) that no sacrifice which man could make would be great enough for the living God. He explained that if the people were to cut down all the trees in the entire land (of Lebanon) and offer all their animals to God, their offering would not be sufficient. (See Isaiah 40:16.)

2. THE PHARISEE SPOKE PROUDLY OF HIMSELF
Matthew 23:1-30; Luke 18:9-12

There are those who think that if a person is good enough, his prayers will be answered. Long, long ago, when the Lord Jesus lived on earth, there was a group of men considered to be good. They were important rulers of the Jewish people, called Pharisees.

The Pharisees did not worship idols of wood, or stone, or silver, or gold. No! They worshiped the true and living God. The Pharisees wore long robes with wide hems so the people would recognize them as they walked down the street or passed through the marketplace. They liked to have people notice them and call out, "Hail, Rabbi!"

Everyone knew that the Pharisees were supposed to be loyal to God and that they studied the laws of God carefully–even adding extra laws of their own. They kept every law strictly. This meant they gave a tenth of their money regularly to God. They refused to touch dead animals. They would not go near a sick person. They believed these things to be against their laws.

The Pharisees studied the Scriptures so they could answer questions that people might ask about the Word of God. They wore, strapped on their foreheads and arms, little leather cases in which were copied parts of Scripture. Oh, they were very religious!

Because these men lived such strict lives, they were given important seats at feasts and in the synagogue. How they liked all the attention the people gave them!

Often these rulers went to the temple to pray. They did not say short prayers and then hurry home. No indeed! Often they said long prayers. (See Matthew 23:1-30.) The Pharisees thought that their prayers pleased God. The people who heard the Pharisees wished they too could utter such prayers. But what did God think of their praying? A story the Lord Jesus told gives the answer.

Show Illustration #2

Jesus said two men went up into the temple to pray. One was a Pharisee and the other was a publican (a tax collector). When the Pharisee walked proudly into the temple to a spot where everyone could see him, he saw the tax collector. Shaking his head he thought to himself, *What a cheater he is! Why does he come into this temple of God? God will never hear his prayer!*

Then, thinking of his own goodness and despising those around him, the Pharisee lifted his head and prayed with himself, "God, I thank You that I am not like other men. I am not greedy, dishonest, impure, or even like that tax collector! I fast twice a week. (That was more than the law required!) I give a tenth part of all that I have."

The Pharisee had finished praying. Had he asked for anything? Did he receive anything? No! He was not really praying to God but only talking proudly with himself.

3. THE TAX COLLECTOR PRAYED HUMBLY TO GOD
Luke 18:13

Show Illustration #3

The Lord Jesus continued the story. He said that the tax collector stepped to a place where he was not noticed. He did not even lift up his head. Rather, he bowed his head low and beat upon his chest, praying, "God, have mercy on me, a sinner." He thought himself to be the chief sinner in the world.

Compared to the prayer of the Pharisee, the tax collector uttered a short prayer. But which prayer do you think was better? Which one did God hear?

4. GOD HEARS THE PRAYERS OF THOSE WHO CONFESS THEIR SINS AND SEEK FORGIVENESS
Luke 18:14

Show Illustration #4

Jesus told the people: "The tax collector went home forgiven by God. (His sinful heart was cleansed.) The Pharisee was not forgiven. (His sin-darkened heart was *not* cleansed.) Everyone who is proud shall be humbled, but the humble (lowly) shall be honored." The Lord Jesus had finished His short story. But the people understood what He was teaching them.

Fine sounding, long prayers are not always the right prayers. It is what is in the heart that matters. The Pharisee was like a cup that was clean on the outside but dirty on the inside. (See Matthew 23:25.) The tax collector, however, cared about the inside. He called on God to clean his heart. Then, because his prayer was answered, his heart was cleansed as a cup that is clean on the inside. This cleansing of the heart is extremely important to God. The Bible says: "If I regard [approve] iniquity [sin] in my heart, the Lord will not hear me" (Psalm 66:18).

The Pharisee had sin in his heart. He was proud. And the Lord did not hear his prayer. The tax collector confessed his sin to God. His prayer was heard and his sin was forgiven. First Peter 3:12 says: "For the eyes of the Lord are over the righteous, and His ears are open unto their prayers; but the face of the Lord is against them that do evil." God, who sees the heart, knew that the seemingly good man, the Pharisee, had great sin: pride. The tax collector, admitting his sin and asking for mercy, is the one God looked upon as "righteous."

What about your prayers? Do you pray to the true God who alone can hear and answer prayer? Have you confessed your sin to God as the tax collector did? Have you asked Him to forgive your sin? If so your sin is forgiven. And you may talk to God about everything, knowing He will hear you.

To be sure you remember these four truths, please write them in your notebook:

1. Prayer is talking to God.
2. Only the true and living God hears and answers prayer.
3. God will hear the prayer of anyone who confesses his sin and seeks forgiveness.
4. When you have been forgiven of your sin, you can talk to God about everything.

Lesson 2
THE MODEL PRAYER

> **NOTE TO THE TEACHER**
>
> When our Lord told the parable of the Pharisee and the publican, there was more teaching than we have included here. Depending on the ability of your students, you may wish to mention two other elements of prayer.
>
> 1. The Word of God clearly teaches that prayer is to be made with thanksgiving. (Read Philippians 4:6.)
>
> Was the Pharisee mindful of this truth when he prayed, "I thank Thee that I am not as other men?" No, he was not. He was simply telling God about his own goodness. This is not thanksgiving. When we thank God for Himself and thank Him for what He has done for us, we offer true thanksgiving.
>
> 2. Believing prayer is answered today because the Lord Jesus Christ gave His blood as a sacrifice for sin. (See Hebrews 10:11-22.)
>
> The publican was an instructed Jew. When he prayed, "God, be merciful to me, a sinner," he was calling to mind that sin must be judged. That judgment is death. From the beginning God, who requires a sacrifice for sin, has accepted a substitute sacrifice (a bird or an animal). It died in place of the sinner. The mercy seat in the Holy of Holies was the place where sin was judged. When the blood of the slain sacrifice was placed on the mercy seat, rather than its being a place of judgment, it became a place of mercy. Instead of being separated from God by his sin, the sinner–because of the substitute sacrifice–could have communion with God. (You should read all about this in Leviticus 16.)
>
> The publican had this in mind when he asked for mercy. He recognized that he needed a sacrifice for his sin and he actually asked God to be his sacrifice! He knew he did not deserve such grace. But God, who is rich in mercy, and who knew the heart of the man, forgave him.

Scripture to be studied: Matthew 6:6-15; 7:7-11; Luke 11:1-13

The *aim* of the lesson: To explain what Jesus taught about prayer.

   What your students should *know*: They may know all the facts about prayer but can only learn to pray by praying.

   What your students should *feel*: Eager to pray.

   What your students should *do*: Learn what to pray for by following the pattern Jesus gave.

Lesson outline (for the teacher's and students' notebooks):

1. Jesus spent much time praying to His Father (Luke 3:21; 6:12; 9:29).
2. Jesus gave His disciples a pattern for praying (Luke 11:1-5).
3. Prayer begins with worshiping God (Matthew 6:9-10).
4. Prayer includes asking God for what we need (Matthew 6:11-15).

The verse to be memorized:

For the eyes of the Lord are over the righteous, and His ears are open unto their prayers. (1 Peter 3:12a)

> **NOTE FOR THE TEACHER**
>
> In the previous lesson, we considered these questions: What is prayer? To whom should we pray? Who can pray? In this lesson you will examine what the Lord Jesus Christ taught about prayer. We have today the perfect example of the prayer life of Christ, together with His pattern for prayer. Pray that the Holy Spirit will apply these truths to the hearts of those you teach so they will know what to pray for.

REVIEW

In our last lesson we learned some important facts about prayer. To whom should we pray? *(To the true and living God in Heaven. He is the only One who can hear and answer prayer.)* Gods of wood, or stone, or silver, or gold cannot hear or answer prayer.

We also learned about two men who went to the temple to pray. Who were they? *(The Pharisee and the tax collector)* Which of these men was a sinner? *(Both were sinners, although the Pharisee did not think he was. The tax collector admitted he was a sinner, he confessed his sin to God, and was forgiven. But the prayer of the Pharisee did not reach God at all.)*

For a person who has never been born again, there is only one prayer he can properly make to God. That is a prayer for forgiveness. The tax collector prayed this kind of prayer. He said, "God, be merciful to me a sinner." When any sinner believes in the Lord Jesus Christ as his Saviour and prays to God for forgiveness (and really means it!) God forgives his sin and makes him His own Child. God is willing to hear the prayers of His children. Only unconfessed sin keeps God from hearing our prayers. (See Psalm 66:18.)

THE LESSON

We get learning in at least two ways. If we want to learn to read and write, we may go to school. There a teacher instructs us and, if we work diligently enough, we soon enjoy reading and writing. But if a girl wishes to learn to cook, she may do so by watching her mother. Before long she can help her mother. And, finally, she is able to cook alone. If a boy wants to learn farming, he watches a farmer, helps a farmer, and soon he knows exactly how to be a good farmer. In a school a girl could study books about cooking. But it is not until she watches and helps with cooking that she really learns to cook. A boy could study many books about farming, without ever knowing really how to farm. He learns to farm by farming.

So it is with prayer. We may be taught certain truths about prayer. Other facts we learn from watching the prayer habits of another. But not until we pray ourselves, do we ever truly learn to pray.

In our lesson today we are going to learn about prayer by looking at Someone else. We shall observe the One whose life was spent almost in constant prayer. Then, too, we shall learn from His lips a pattern that will help us as we pray.

Please keep your notebook before you so you can immediately write down each fact that you learn about prayer.

1. JESUS SPENT MUCH TIME PRAYING TO HIS FATHER
Luke 3:21; 6:12; 9:29

Do you ever wish that you could have been right with the Lord Jesus when He was here on earth? I do. Because that is impossible, we can do the next best thing: *imagine* we were with Him. On certain illustrations in this lesson you will see big dots. Each dot represents you. You are right there! Listen carefully; watch closely. See if you can learn what God the Son wants you to know about prayer.

Show Illustration #5a

At the beginning of His ministry, the Lord Jesus was baptized in the Jordan River. That very moment Jesus was praying to God the Father. (See Luke 3:21.) The words He spoke in that prayer are not recorded. But we learn this important truth: Before preaching a sermon or performing a miracle–the Lord Jesus prayed. He, God the Son, was teaching us that *all service for God must begin with prayer to God.*

Show Illustration #5b

If you are alert, you will quickly learn the next truth about prayer.

It was time for the Lord Jesus to choose His 12 disciples. This was of tremendous importance. The disciples were to be with Him for three years of ministry. It was to them He would give the work of God after three years. God the Son had to know the will of God His Father.

So the Lord Jesus "went out into a mountain to pray, and continued all night in prayer to God" (Luke 6:12).

Here, then, is another fact about prayer to be written in your notebook–and to be practiced: *to know the will of God, spend much time alone with God.*

Show Illustration #5c

Listen carefully to learn another important truth about prayer.

The Lord Jesus took three disciples–Peter, James, and John–with Him up into a mountain. There He prayed. Although He was God from all eternity, yet He had chosen to become Man. As Man, He was dependent upon the Father. He loved to talk with His Father. On this occasion, as He prayed His face was changed and His clothes became "white and glistening" (Luke 9:29). In a most unusual way the beauty and glory of the Lord God shone from Him.

What additional truth do we learn from this? *Our lives are changed and the beauty of the Lord our God is upon us when we spend time with Him in prayer.*

2. JESUS GAVE HIS DISCIPLES A PATTERN FOR PRAYING
Luke 11:1-5

Show Illustration #6

One day as Jesus was praying, the disciples realized that their own prayers were not what they should be. So one of them said, "Lord, teach us to pray."

Before doing so, the Lord Jesus warned, "When you pray, do not use vain repetitions, as the heathen do: for they think they shall be heard for their much speaking" (Matthew 6:7). Real prayer is talking to God as simply as a child talks to his father. And the Son of God Himself forbids us to repeat meaningless, empty prayers.

So they would have a pattern for knowing how to speak to God and what requests are to be made to Him, Jesus taught them (and us!): "After this manner you should pray: 'Our Father who art in Heaven, Hallowed be Thy name. Thy kingdom come. Thy will be done in earth, as it is in Heaven. Give us this day our daily bread. And forgive us our debts, as we forgive our debtors. And lead us not into temptation, but deliver us from evil.'"

It is such a short prayer that we could easily memorize it and say it almost without thinking. Instead, it is a prayer that teaches us to pray. What does it teach us? It teaches at least *six matters which should be in our prayers.*

3. PRAYER BEGINS WITH WORSHIPING GOD
Matthew 6:9-10

The first part of the prayer has to do with God Himself.

Show Illustration #7a

1. True Prayer begins with *worship and adoration.*

When a child of God talks to His Father in Heaven, he worships Him–honors Him–by speaking reverently and lovingly to Him: "Our Father who art in Heaven." Even though we cannot see Him, we speak to Him with great respect. When we say "Hallowed [holy] be Thy name," we are remembering that God is perfect in holiness and therefore without sin. Because of who He is, we regard Him with love and respect. (See John 17:1, 11, 25.) We should bow in worship and adoration of Him before we ask anything for ourselves.

Show Illustration #7b

2. We should pray *about the future.*

There is a day coming when the kingdom of God will be set up here on earth. That kingdom will be made up of all who acknowledge the Lord Jesus Christ as the Son of God and their Saviour. When we pray, "Thy kingdom come," we should remember our responsibility to tell others the good news of salvation. (See Revelation 22:20.)

Show Illustration #7c

3. We should pray *that we shall know and do the will of God.*

There is joy in Heaven because those who are there do the will of God. When we on earth do the will of God, we too have great joy. If we are perfectly willing to do whatever God wants us to do, we pray, "Thy will be done on earth as it is in Heaven."

4. PRAYER INCLUDES ASKING GOD FOR WHAT WE NEED
Matthew 6:11-15

While the first part of the prayer has to do with God, the rest of the prayer has to do with ourselves.

Show Illustration #8a

4. Prayer includes asking *for daily needs*.

We are to depend upon God–our loving, living Father–for all the needs of life: "Give us this day our daily bread." He supplies our needs as we ask Him definitely for them. (See also Matthew 6:33; Philippians 4:6-7.) (Bread, in the days of the Lord Jesus, was doubtless round and flat.)

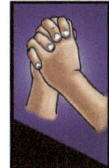

Show Illustration #8b

5. Prayer includes *forgiving others* and *asking forgiveness for our sin*.

Even after we are born again into the family of God, we do wrong things. When we pray, we are to confess those sins and ask forgiveness. (See 1 John 1:9.) Because God forgives our sins, we are to forgive others–even those who have wronged us most. So our prayer should be, "Forgive us our debts [sins] as we forgive our debtors [those who sin against us]."

Show Illustration #8c

6. *We should ask to be kept from sin* when we pray.

We know we have weaknesses that cause us to sin. So we are to ask God to keep us from becoming overpowered by Satan. That is why we ask: "And lead us not into temptation but deliver us from [the] evil [one]." The Lord Jesus can hold back the forces of evil and darkness and can keep His children from sin. He will do so when we ask Him for victory. (See 1 Corinthians 10:13.)

This pattern for prayer was given to the disciples and to the Jewish people who lived in that day. But it is an equally good pattern for Christians today. It is important to pray with understanding and to pray from the heart. You do not need to use the exact words. You should avoid "vain repetitions"– saying words without meaning them. But you should pray that:

1. The name of God will be honored.
2. The kingdom of God will come.
3. The will of God will be done.

And you should pray for:

4. Your needs.
5. Forgiveness of sin.
6. Victory over temptation.

Remember! It is possible to know all these facts without knowing how to pray. You will learn to pray only one way: by praying.

> **NOTE TO THE TEACHER**
> You will observe that in Matthew the prayer closes with: "For Thine is the kingdom, and the power, and the glory forever." Because this is not in the best original texts and was added later, we have not included it here.

Lesson 3
THE PERSISTENT FRIEND AND THE PERSISTENT WIDOW

Scripture to be studied: Luke 11:5-13; Matthew 7:7-11; Luke 18:1-8

The *aim* of the lesson: To teach your students how to pray.

What your students should *know*: Sometimes God does not answer our prayers because we are asking for the wrong thing.

What your students should *feel*: Encouraged to continue praying.

What your students should *do*: Pray with persistence.

Lesson outline (for the teacher's and students' notebooks):

1. Prayer is asking without stopping (Luke 11:5-7).
2. Those who keep on asking, receive (Luke 11:8-13).
3. Prayer should be continued until an answer comes (Luke 18:1-3).
4. Faith is rewarded by answered prayer (Luke 18:4-8).

The verse to be memorized:

For the eyes of the Lord are over the righteous, and His ears are open unto their prayers. (1 Peter 3:12a)

REVIEW QUESTIONS

1. What is prayer? *(Talking to God)*
2. To whom should we pray? *(To the true and living God)*
3. Who can pray? *(Every person can pray for forgiveness of sin. Only the children of God can rightly call God their Heavenly Father and they can pray about everything.)*
4. For what should children of God pray?
   a. That the name of God will be honored.
   b. That the kingdom of God will come soon.
   c. That the will of God will be done on earth as it is done in Heaven.
   d. *For our needs.*
   e. *For forgiveness.*
   f. *For victory over temptation.*

> **NOTE TO THE TEACHER**
> In the last two lessons, you have taught *to whom* we should pray, *who* can pray and *what* to pray. Now you will teach *how* to pray. The two stories in this lesson illustrate the truth that we should persist (refuse to give up) in prayer, having faith that God will answer even though there may be long delays.
>
> Do you really believe God when He says: "Call unto Me and I will answer thee and show thee great and mighty things which thou knowest not"? Do you believe in the power of prayer? If you do, you can teach this lesson from your heart and from your own experience.
>
> Teacher, please make it clear to your students that often we have to add certain details in stories–details which are not included in the Bible narrative. There is no way of our knowing *exactly* what people thought and said, but we believe they probably said and thought and acted as indicated in these stories.

THE LESSON

1. PRAYER IS ASKING WITHOUT STOPPING
Luke 11:5-7

Immediately after teaching His disciples the manner in which to pray, the Lord Jesus taught an important truth about prayer. And He taught it by telling this story:

Show Illustration #9

Knock! knock! knock! (*Teacher,* knock a few times on a hard surface.) In the middle of the night, the father of the house was awakened by a knock on his door. He was sleepy. He did not feel like getting up, so he closed his eyes and tried to go back to sleep. *Knock! knock! knock!* There it was again–that loud knock. Who could it be? Why would anyone be knocking at this hour (midnight)? Everyone should be in bed. The father lay quietly. His children were asleep also. He did not want them to wake up. *If only that person at the door would go away, I could go back to sleep,* he thought.

Right then there was another knock–louder than before. And a man called out, "Please, lend me three loaves of bread." It was the voice of his neighbor.

I wish he would be quiet, the father thought. *He will wake up my children. Why does he need bread in the middle of the night?*

His neighbor called again: "A friend of mine lost his way and has just come to my house. He is hungry. And I have nothing to give him. Please, will you help me?"

Still the father did not want to answer the door. *I wish he would go back home,* he thought, *or go ask someone else. I want to go back to sleep.* Then he called out crossly, "Do not bother me! You can see the door is locked for the night. My children and I are all in bed. I cannot help you!"

Now he could turn over and go to sleep.

But he did not sleep. His neighbor did not go away. He kept knocking–again, and again, and again.

Why does he keep knocking? the father wondered. *Why does he keep waiting and waiting? Will he never give up?*

2. THOSE WHO KEEP ON ASKING, RECEIVE
Luke 11:8-13

At last he could stand it no longer. He got up as quietly as possible, lighted a lamp, tiptoed to the cupboard and got three loaves of bread. He unlocked the door.

Show Illustration #10

His friend was still waiting. Quickly he gave him the bread.

"Thank you, thank you, my friend!" the neighbor exclaimed.

Now the father could go back to bed and to sleep.

When the Lord Jesus finished telling this story to His disciples, He explained, "This is the way it is with prayer. Keep on asking and you will receive. Keep on seeking and you will keep finding. Keep on knocking and the door will be opened. For the one who asks will always receive, one who is searching will always find, and the door will be opened to the man who knocks."

What did the Lord Jesus mean? He meant that because prayer is such a simple exercise, we might think that all we have to do is to ask God for whatever we want and immediately He will give it to us. Because of that we might ask for things which are not good for us. Or perhaps, after receiving what we asked for, we really would not want it. So as we pray, asking God for that which we desire, we may have to ask repeatedly. In our constant asking, we shall start seeking what is His will. We shall search our hearts to be certain that if we receive that which we ask for, it will bring glory to our Father God. His delay in giving what we ask may cause us to realize that we were asking for something that would be wrong for us to have. Or if we have received it, we may have become quite proud. Pride is sin. And we should judge our sin as we pray. When we ask, seeking the will of God, we can be certain He will supply every need.

Jesus, after telling the story of the persistent neighbor, added, "Some of you are fathers. If your son asks for bread, will you give him a stone?" (The flat, round bread of Jesus' day could easily be mistaken for a stone.) The men must have thought, *Of course not. I would never trick my son and give him a stone when he asked for bread.*

Jesus continued, "If a son asks for a fish (for food) would you give him a snake (which would kill him)?"

The fathers knew the answer to this.

"If your son asked for an egg [to eat]," Jesus added, "would you give him a scorpion [which would destroy him]?"

Of course not!

"Then," Jesus explained, "if you, as bad as you are, know how to give to your children what is good for them, how much more will your heavenly Father give good things to those who ask Him!"

God, our heavenly Father, is not like the father who did not want to be bothered by his neighbor. God wants His children to come to Him again and again in prayer. He wants us to keep on asking for the things we need and want–for the things that will bring glory to Him. He knows what is best for us and will give us all that is right for us in His time, if we keep asking.

3. PRAYER SHOULD BE CONTINUED UNTIL AN ANSWER COMES
Luke 18:1-3

On another day, the Lord Jesus told the disciples another story to remind them of the importance of praying without ceasing. Here is the story:

Show Illustration #11

There was once a woman who was in great trouble. Her husband had died and an evil man was trying to harm her. *If only my husband were living,* she thought, *he would protect me and keep me safe from this evil man. I am terrified of him. What can I do? Who can help me?* Then she had an idea. *I shall go to the judge of the city. I shall tell him about this enemy who wants to hurt me. He will do something to protect me from this awful man.*

In those days a judge usually sat inside the gate of the city and anyone could come to him for justice.

As the frightened widow hurried toward the city gate, she watched this way and that to make certain her enemy was not following her.

Her heart beat fast as she approached the judge. *He will protect me,* she thought.

4. FAITH IS REWARDED BY ANSWERED PRAYER
Luke 18:4-8

Show Illustration #12

She told him about her enemy and begged, "Please protect me. Please!"

The judge answered her roughly and told her there was nothing he could do. "Go away!" he demanded.

Sadly, the woman went home. She was still afraid. She knew she was not safe. "I *must* get protection," she said. "I shall go back to the judge. Perhaps he will change his mind."

She hurried back to the city gate. Again she begged the judge, "Help me! Please help me!"

The judge exclaimed, "Go away! I told you before I could not help you."

Once again the woman turned toward home. But she was not willing to give up. Again she bravely went to the judge and pleaded with him.

At last the judge could stand it no longer. "All right. All right!" he shouted. "It is true I do not fear God or man. But this woman bothers me. She is a great nuisance. I shall see that she gets justice before she wears me out by coming again and again."

Jesus concluded His story by saying, "You heard what the evil judge said. Do you suppose that God, as patient as He is, will not give justice to His people who plead with Him day and night? Yes, He will answer them. But the question is, When the Son of Man comes, will He find men on earth who believe on Him?" (Or will they stop believing when the answer to their prayer takes a long time to come?)

Whenever the disciples thought of that story they must have remembered what the Lord Jesus said when He began it. "Men ought always to pray and not to faint [not to stop until an answer comes]" (Luke 18:1).

The Lord Jesus told both stories so we would remember this very important truth: We are to pray with persistence. Pray, believing that God *will* answer. Keep on praying and seeking His will and believing, even though it may take a long time for the answer to come. God knows what is best for you–and *when* it is best for you.

Lesson 4
PRAYER

NOTE TO THE TEACHER

The first three lessons in this series established certain truths about prayer. Now we shall teach *when to pray* and *where to praay*. Also included are a few simple rules for prayer and a list of those *for whom we should pray.*

Prayerlessness is sin. (See 1 Samuel 12:23.) Pray and teach so earnestly that each one in your class will learn to pray effectively. Those who are members of the family of God through faith in the Lord Jesus Christ should approach Him in childlike simplicity. He, our divine Father, is great, eternal, good. He is love. We, His children, should be reverent and trusting, simply telling Him our needs, our longings, our love. We should thank Him in worship and adoration for Himself, His gifts, His blessings, His care.

If you enjoy your prayer life, your students will want to follow your example. (See 1 Peter 5:2-3.)

The *aim* of the lesson: To teach your students: (1) When to pray, (2) Where to pray, (3) Rules for prayer, (4) For whom we should pray.

What your students should *know*: God desires to hear our prayers, but Satan wants to keep us from praying.

What your students should *feel*: Determined to pray even though Satan will try to stop them.

What your students should *do*: Set a definite time for prayer.

Lesson outline (for the teacher's and students' notebooks):

1. The right times to pray (Luke 6:12; Mark 1:35; 6:46; Psalm 55:17; 1 Thessalonians 5:17).
2. The right places to pray (Matthew 6:6).
3. Rules for prayer (1 John 5:14-15; John 14:13-14; Philippians 4:6).
4. For whom we should pray.

The verse to be memorized:

For the eyes of the Lord are over the righteous, and His ears are open unto their prayers. (1 Peter 3:12a)

THE LESSON

Our God is not like other gods. He is not like gods of gold, silver, wood, or stone. He is not like the sun god or the moon god. In fact, the true and living God of Heaven made the sun and the moon, the gold, the silver, the wood and stone. Our God is Creator of everything. He made the mighty oceans, the high mountains, the huge trees, the strongest animals. He made every drop of water, each tiny snowflake, every grain of sand, even the smallest insect. (See Job 36:27; Psalm 147:16.) He made the grass, the flowers, the birds. But most wonderful of all, He made you and He made me.

Of everything God made, He loves people the most. It is hard for us to imagine that One so great and wise and good as God could care about us and love us. But He does. Because He loves us so much, He wants to talk to us through His Word, the Bible. And He wants us to talk to Him. Talking to God is *prayer.*

People have many different ideas about prayer. To some, the name of God is a charm against evil. They believe that if they simply say the name of God they will be safe from harm. Others believe that every mention of the name of God is counted as a separate prayer. So they repeat His name over and over again from morning until night.

Some people use a string of beads or pearls or berries when they pray. Each time a prayer or the name of their god is repeated, they move one bead on the string. In this way they keep count of the number of prayers they make. The string may have as many as 50 or 100 beads on it.

– 25 –

When there are such different ideas about prayer, how can we know for sure what real prayer is? How can we answer such questions as: *When is the right time to pray? Where is the right place to pray? What are the rules of prayer? For whom should we pray?*

The Bible gives us the answers to these questions. And because the Bible is the Word of God, it is true. So let us see what the Bible has to tell us about prayer.

1. THE RIGHT TIMES TO PRAY
Luke 6:12; Mark 1:35; 6:46;
Psalm 55:17; 1 Thessalonians 5:17

When is the right time to pray?

Without answering this question directly, the Lord Jesus *showed* us by His practice when we should pray.

Show Illustration #13a

We are told that "He went out into a mountain to pray, and continued all night in prayer to God" (Luke 6:12). He had to be certain of the will of God, for the next day He would choose His 12 disciples. In the quiet of night He talked to His Father. Nighttime is indeed a good time to pray.

Show Illustration #13b

On another occasion we read, "In the morning, rising up a great while before day, He went out, and departed into a solitary place, and there prayed" (Mark 1:35). In the darkness the Lord Jesus made His way to a quiet place where–in the first light of dawn–He could talk alone to God. It was to be an unusually busy day. It would be a tiring day. For that very reason He arose early. He would need the strength and wisdom God would give Him in answer to His early morning prayer. (See Isaiah 40:28-31).

Show Illustration #13c

At another time Jesus sent everyone away and "He departed into a mountain to pray" (Mark 6:46). What time was this? At the close of a busy day. There had been sad news. John the Baptist (a friend of Jesus) had been murdered by King Herod. Jesus and His disciples had crossed the lake in a boat. He had spent most of the day teaching thousands of people. Then He had performed a glorious miracle: feeding 5,000 men (besides women and children), using the little lunch of a young boy. It had been an exhausting day. (See Mark 6:14-46.) But the Son of God closed the day in prayer to His Father.

One who had lived hundreds of years before the Lord Jesus wrote in the Word of God : ". . . Evening, and morning, and at noon, will I pray . . ." (Psalm 55:17). And the command to us is: "Pray without ceasing" (1 Thessalonians 5:17).

When is the right time to pray? Any time of day or night. (See Psalm 139:1-12.) We should pray when we are afraid. We should pray when we are sick and when we are happy. We should pray when it comes our time to die. God is never too busy to listen to His own people. And, because God is so great and powerful, He can hear the prayers of all His children, even if they all pray at the same time!

2. THE RIGHT PLACES TO PRAY
Matthew 6:6

Our God–the true and living God–is everywhere at once. (See Psalm 139; Proverbs 15:3.) There is not one place where God cannot hear you, and He will hear you if your heart is right toward Him (cleansed of sin). You can pray wherever you are.

Show Illustration #14a

The publican prayed in the temple. We can certainly pray in church and in other public places, where we may be surrounded by people.

Show Illustration #14b

The Lord Jesus prayed alone on the mountain. It is important that we have times when we are apart from others when we pray.

Show Illustration #14c

When instructing His disciples about prayer, the Lord Jesus began, "You, when you pray, enter into your room, and when you have shut the door, pray to your Father who is in secret; and your Father who sees in secret will reward you openly." (See Matthew 6:6.)

It's necessary to have a special, quiet place where you talk to God alone at definite times each day. Have you set such a place?

In earlier lessons we have observed that when we pray we are to *worship God, ask for the will of God, confess our sins,* and *pray with a forgiving heart.* Let us add now a few more rules for prayer. (You are writing these in your notebook, I trust.)

3. RULES FOR PRAYER
1 John 5:14-15; John 14:13-14; Philippians 4:6

(1) *We are to pray in faith.* (See Matthew 21:22; 1 John 5:14-15.)

We are to believe God and trust in Him, knowing His answer (whether it is "yes" or "no" or "wait") is best.

Show Illustration #15a

A young man who had recently been saved was making his first public prayer. When he came to the end, he did not know how to conclude. Then, stretching out his hands, he ended, "Expecting to hear from You soon." He prayed with faith.

Show Illustration #15b

(2) *We are to pray in the name of Jesus.* (**Teacher:** Read John 14:13-14 to your students.)

When we pray in the name of Jesus, it means we are in the presence of God because of what Jesus has done for us–not because we are good in ourselves. Our sins are cleansed by His precious blood.

(3) *We are to pray with praise and thanksgiving.* (See Philippians 4:6.)

Prayer is not simply asking for things. Take time to adore God and to thank Him for all that He is and for all He has done. Tell Him you love Him.

4. FOR WHOM WE SHOULD PRAY

Show Illustration #16

So we shall always remember for whom to pray, let us name them according to our fingers (taken from *No Common Task,* by George Reindrop).

1. The thumb, which is nearest the body, stands for those who are near and dear to us: our family–father, mother, grandparents (do you see them at the top of the illustration?), close friends, people we are with every day. We pray for them.

2. The second finger, called "the pointer," is the one which reminds us to pray for those who point to the cross of Jesus and tell the way of salvation–pastors, Sunday school teachers, evangelists, missionaries.

3. The third finger, the tallest, reminds us of those who are in high places of authority–kings and leaders of our country and community. God has commanded that we pray for them (1 Timothy 2:2).

4. The fourth finger is usually the weakest. So it reminds us to pray for all who are sick, or poor, or in trouble. (Do you see the one who is lying down, ill?–and the one with the bandaged sore leg?)

5. The little finger reminds us to pray for ourselves.

Satan, the enemy of God and our enemy, wants to keep you from praying. He does not want you to believe God. Do not give in to his tricks! Set definite times for prayer. And make it the habit of your life to walk and talk with God. (***Teacher:*** Read Psalm 37:3-7.)

www.ingramcontent.com/pod-product-compliance
Lightning Source LLC
Chambersburg PA
CBHW060805090426
42736CB00002B/160